100 Wa

Elizabeth Fil
Midlands
Aberystwyth University, then in 1983 became a trainee journalist with the *Birmingham Post and Mail*. She has continued to work in journalism, mainly in a freelance capacity. At first, she specialized in writing about sport, but since 1990 has turned her hand to other subjects, including eating disorders, travel, women's issues and contemporary Christianity.

Other titles by Elizabeth Filleul in the same series available from Marshall Pickering

100 WAYS TO BE AT PEACE
100 WAYS TO SHARE THE GOOD NEWS
100 WAYS TO PRAY MORE EFFECTIVELY

100 Ways
TO INCREASE
YOUR FAITH

Elizabeth Filleul

Marshall Pickering

An Imprint of HarperCollins*Publishers*

Marshall Pickering is an Imprint of
HarperCollins*Religious*
Part of HarperCollins*Publishers*
77–85 Fulham Palace Road, London W6 8JB

First published in Great Britain
in 1995 by Marshall Pickering

1   3   5   7   9   10   8   6   4   2

A catalogue record for this book is
available from the British Library

ISBN 0 557 02964-1

Printed and bound in Great Britain by
Woolnough Bookbinding Limited,
Irthlingborough, Northamptonshire

CONDITIONS OF SALE

Introduction

'IT is a good thing to read books of quotations …. The quotations, when engraved upon the memory, give you good thoughts. They also make you anxious to read the authors and look for more.' So claimed Sir Winston Churchill in his autobiography *My Early Life: A Roving Commission*. And his appreciation of wise and witty quotations seems to be shared by a lot of people these days, judging by the number of anthologies on sale in bookshops.

100 Ways to Increase Your Faith is a book of quotations with a difference. It is intended for the Christian wishing to deepen their relationship with God, to walk more closely with Jesus Christ, and to live by his commandments.

What do we mean by 'faith'? According to the *BBC English Dictionary* it is 'a strong religious belief'. If you *have faith* in someone or something, it says, you 'feel confident about their ability or goodness'. As Christians, we have faith in the redemptive power of Jesus Christ. We believe that in committing our lives to him, we are reconciled to God. We believe that when we die, we shall go to heaven to be with him. And we believe that, while on earth, we can have a personal relationship with him.

From the moment a person becomes a Christian, there are opportunities for them to develop their relationship with God and to deepen their faith. This book outlines 100 ways in which Christians can do just that. Here are just a few examples of what that might mean:

- Faith means recognizing that your own lack of revival may be to blame for lack of revival in your church.

- Faith means accepting all peoples in the world as your brother and sister, regardless of race or culture.

- Faith is recognizing that Christianity does not end with your conversion.

- Faith is doing whatever good you can whenever you can.

- Faith is recognizing that building your relationship with God involves work – Bible study, prayer, meditation.

- Faith is doing things because you love God rather than because you enjoy the admiration of others.

- Faith is using, not hiding, the gifts that God has given you.

- Faith is casting aside your troubles and concerns and relaxing in the presence of God.

- Faith is surrendering everything you possess – your family, friends, money, material possessions, skills, talents – to God.

- Faith is setting your heart on knowing Jesus better in the same way you might set your heart on a new romance or job.

Faith, then, is an ongoing process. Whatever we know about God, there will always be more to learn. And one way of learning is by discovering what people down the ages have found out about God in their own spiritual journeys. This book contains ideas from ancient and contemporary spiritual leaders, teachers and writers. I urge you to go on to read their work, to uncover even more ways to know God more intimately and to increase your faith.

The selected quotations show tremendous variety in strategies for increasing your faith. I have my personal favourites; you will too. What will become clear is that there is no single suggestion that is appropriate for every individual at any one time. Much will depend upon your individual personality and your spiritual experience to date.

Each quotation is accompanied by a suggestion for reflection or practical action. Some suggestions take the form of a question, inviting you to scrutinize aspects of your spiritual life, to discover where you might make a progression or pin-point when your faith began to stagnate.

This book is not a 'step-by-step' guide to instant holiness. The Christian life is not like that. But, by following the advice, you will find yourself thinking more deeply about your own spiritual life, its progression, and about the God you serve and worship. What is important to remember, though, is that the journey of faith will last a lifetime and that it is meant to be both challenging and enjoyable. In the words of William of St Thierry:

Lord, I am a countryman
coming from my country to yours.
Teach me the laws of your country,
its way of life, its spirit,
so that I may feel at home there.

IT is very important for us to associate with others who are walking in the right way – not only those who are where we are in the journey, but also those who have gone farther.

Those who have drawn close to God have the ability to bring us closer to him, for in a sense they take us with them.

ST TERESA OF AVILA, *The Interior Castle*

🕯 Invite a more mature Christian round for coffee or a meal this week. Ask them to tell you some of the lessons they have learned in their Christian life.

Don't compromise

WHEN he [Jesus] said 'Be perfect', he meant it. He meant that we must go in for the full treatment. It is hard; but the sort of compromise we are all hankering after is harder – in fact, it is impossible. It may be hard for an egg to turn into a bird: it would be a jolly sight harder for it to learn to fly while remaining an egg. We are like eggs at present. And you cannot go on indefinitely being just an ordinary, decent egg. We must be hatched, or go bad!

C.S. LEWIS, *Mere Christianity*

❧ In which areas of your life is your faith being compromised? Today, choose one of those areas and make sure other people know exactly where you stand spiritually.

WHAT good is it, my brothers and sisters, if you say you have faith but do not have works? Can faith save you? If a brother or sister is naked and lacks daily food, and one of you says to them, 'Go in peace, keep warm and eat your fill,' and yet you do not supply their bodily needs, what is the good of that? So faith by itself, if it has no works, is dead.

JAMES 2:14–17

> 🐚 This week, donate money, food or clothing to a charity which helps the poor at home or abroad. Consider making this a regular commitment.

Be like a child

A child is a natural contemplative, constantly wondering *at*. For children, everything is laden with aesthetic and supernatural dimensions. Only later, when we approach reality with more and more *a priori* filters, do we begin to see less and less of the aesthetic and the supernatural.

RONALD ROLHEISER, *The Shattered Lantern*

❧ Do something you enjoyed as a child – play on the swings in the park, paint a picture, read a favourite childhood book. Remember the emotions and wonder you felt as a child – where everything was new and exciting. How did you relate to God then? What does that tell you about how you might relate to God now?

A little girl was kneeling on her father's lap and telling him how much she loved him, but she was looking over her father's shoulder and making faces at her little brother. The mother saw it and said: 'You little hypocrite, you telling your father you love him and then making faces at your little brother.' Christians who hold race prejudices do just that. They tell God the Father they love him and then look over his shoulder and tell his other children they despise them. How can we love God whom we have not seen unless we love his children whom we do see?

E. STANLEY JONES, Conversion

🔖 Is there a person or a group of people you despise? Remember, they, like you, are God's children. Picture them in your mind and address them as 'brother' or 'sister'. Get to know about them and their situation and then re-examine your opinion.

Don't fear God

WHAT folly to fear to be too entirely God's! It is to fear to be too happy. It is to fear to have too much courage in the crosses which are inevitable, too much comfort in God's love, and too much detachment from the passions which make us miserable.

FRANÇOIS FÉNELON, *Christian Perfection*

❦ List some of the feelings and fears you would experience, as well as the good things you would miss out on, if you were not completely committed to God.

Appreciate Jesus' humiliation and pain

WE were lined up in the hospital corridor for medical inspection. We had to remove all our clothes and lay them on the floor of the entrance hall. Never in my life had I felt so wretched, so cold, or so humiliated.

Suddenly I recalled a painting of Jesus on Golgotha. For the first time I realized that Jesus had hung naked upon the cross. How he must have suffered! He, God's son, whose home was heaven! And all that suffering he bore for me, that I might some day go to heaven.

My soul became calm within me. I felt that strength was given me to go on. I prayed, 'O Saviour, thou didst suffer for me on Calvary. I thank thee for it. Help me now to bear this present experience. Give me strength!'

CORRIE TEN BOOM, *A Prisoner and Yet*

❧ Think of Jesus hanging naked on a cross – for you. Think of the pain and humiliation he suffered – for you. Thank him for it, and recall it when you need it most.

Let God draw close to you

IN prayer God meets us in our humanity, and the work of transforming that humanity into divinity is his. I can give all I possess to the poor, visit the sick, never step out of line or ever commit a serious sin, but I can be a million miles from God and not be letting him anywhere near me because I am caught up in the pride of achievement.

DELIA SMITH, *A Journey Into God*

🐾 Do you feel miles away from God, in spite of all your Christian activities? Pray, and draw close to him – and allow him to come close to you.

Do not despise or run down any preacher. Do not exalt anyone above the rest lest you hurt both him and the cause of God. Do not bear hard upon any preacher because of some inconsistency or inaccuracy of expression; no, not even for some mistake, not even if you are right.

Do not even give a single thought of separating from your brethren, whether their opinions agree with yours or not. Just because someone does not agree with everything you say does not mean they are sinning.

JOHN WESLEY, *Christian Perfection*

🐾 If you disagree with your pastor or someone in your fellowship, don't cause divisions by voicing your views. Always seek reconciliation rather than division.

Forgive and forget

O Lord Jesus, because, being full of foolishness, we often sin and have to ask pardon, help us to forgive as we would be forgiven; neither mentioning old offences committed against us, nor dwelling upon them in thought, nor being influenced by them in heart, but loving our brother freely, as you freely loved us.

CHRISTINA ROSSETTI

❧ Have you outwardly forgiven someone for something – but frequently find yourself brooding on, or mentioning, the offence? Resolve to dismiss it from your mind.

Learn from Bible characters

Y o u who guided Noah over the flood waves:
hear us.
You who with your word recalled Jonah from the deep:
deliver us.
You who stretched forth your hand to Peter as he sank:
help us, O Christ.
Son of God, who did marvellous things of old:
be favourable in our day also.

Scots Celtic Prayer

❧ Read about the life of a Bible character today. Let
the knowledge of the way God helped them deepen
your own faith.

Observe all commandments

FOR if Christianity teaches anything about eating and drinking, spending our time and money, how we are to live in the world, what attitudes we are to have in daily life, how we are to be disposed toward all people, how we are to behave toward the sick, the poor, the old, and destitute, whom we are to treat with particular love, whom we are to regard with a particular esteem, how we are to treat our enemies, and how we are to deny ourselves, we would be foolish to think that these teachings are not to be observed with the same strictness as those teachings that relate to prayer.

WILLIAM LAW,
A Serious Call to a Devout and Holy Life

❧ Which of Jesus' commandments in the gospels do you fail to keep? Act on one of them straight away, and resolve to pay as much attention to it as you do to your prayer life.

BUT this eternal and overflowing love does not come when I am relaxing, nor do I feel this spiritual ardour when I am tired out after, say, travelling; nor is it [there] when I am absorbed with worldly interests or engrossed in never-ending arguments. At times like these I catch myself growing cold: cold until once again I put away all things external, and make a real effort to stand in my Saviour's presence; only then do I abide in this inner warmth.

RICHARD ROLLE, *The Fire of Love*

For a while, forget everything that is going on around you, and all your internal worries and cares, and concentrate only on being in God's presence.

Be amazed

I T is amazing that a poor human creature is able to speak with God's high majesty in heaven and not be afraid.

MARTIN LUTHER, *Table Talk*

🐾 Think of someone in authority or who you admire who you would be nervous of approaching. What does the fact that the creator of the universe listens to you say about him and his love? Let the lesson settle deep inside you.

Let God use everything

L ET me then put back into your hand all that you have given me, rededicating to your service all the powers of my mind and body, all my worldly goods, all my influence with others. All these, O Father, are yours to use as you will.

JOHN BAILLIE, *A Diary of Private Prayer*

🐾 Is there anything in your life – e.g. any material possessions, a talent or a relationship – which is not under God's control? Today, surrender it to him.

Be eager

IT ought to be tremendously helpful to be able to acquire the habit of reaching out strongly after God's thoughts, and to ask, 'God, what have you to put in my mind now if only I can be large enough?' That waiting, eager attitude ought to give God the chance he needs.

FRANK LAUBACH, *Letters by a Modern Mystic*

❧ Give God the chance he needs to work in you by praying this prayer – now.

See yourself as an answer to prayer

You may pray for the release of some area of life in a friend and find that you are called upon to set right something in your own life that has acted as a stumbling block to him. You may pray that your friend be given courage to endure certain hardships and find that you are drawn to pack your bag and go with him or that you are to give up your pocket money for the next month or even perhaps to give a fortnight's or a month's salary to help along his cause. In intercessory prayer one seldom ends where one began.

DOUGLAS V. STEERE, *Prayer and Worship*

    🐾 Have you ever prayed for someone else and realized that you needed to do something for that prayer to be answered? The next time you intercede for someone, remind yourself that the answer may lie with you.

Know what time it is

FOR everything there is a season, and a time for every
   matter under heaven:
a time to be born, and a time to die;
a time to plant, and a time to pluck up what is planted;
a time to kill, and a time to heal;
a time to break down, and a time to build up;
a time to weep, and a time to laugh;
a time to mourn, and a time to dance;
a time to throw away stones, and a time to gather
   stones together;
a time to embrace, and a time to refrain from
   embracing;
a time to seek, and a time to lose;
a time to keep, and a time to throw away;
a time to tear, and a time to sew;
a time to keep silence, and a time to speak;
a time to love, and a time to hate;
a time for war, and a time for peace.
ECCLESIASTES 3:1–8

🍃 What is the 'time' in your life now? If you are
mourning, remind yourself that there will be a time to
dance; if weeping, a time to laugh.

Look for potential beauty

I asked the Lord
for a bunch of fresh flowers
but instead he gave me an ugly cactus
with many thorns.
I asked the Lord
for some beautiful butterflies
but instead he gave me
many ugly and dreadful worms.
I was threatened,
I was disappointed,
I mourned,
but after many days,
suddenly,
I saw the cactus bloom
with many beautiful flowers,
and those worms became
beautiful butterflies
flying in the spring wind.
God's way is the best way.

CHUN-MING KAO

❧ Look for potential beauty in anything God has
given you with which you feel dissatisfied.

Don't gossip

I wonder why we are so eager to chatter and gossip with each other, since we seldom return to the quiet of our own hearts without a damaged conscience? The reason is that by idle chit-chat we seek comfort from one another and we hope to lighten our distracted hearts. And to make matters worse, we chatter most freely about our favourite topics, about what we would like to have, or about those things we especially dislike!

What a mistake! This outside comfort is no small detriment to the inner comfort that comes from God. Therefore, we must watch and pray that we do not waste time. If it is proper to speak, speak of what will benefit others spiritually. Bad habits and neglect of our spiritual progress contribute much to our endless chatter.

THOMAS À KEMPIS, *The Imitation of Christ*

❦ Avoid joining in and listening to gossip. If you find yourself caught up in it, pause and inwardly pray for the strength not to continue.

AFTER a soul has been converted by God, that soul is nurtured and caressed by the Spirit. Like a loving mother, God cares for and comforts the infant soul by feeding it spiritual milk. Such souls will find great delight in this stage. They will begin praying with great urgency and perseverance; they will engage in all kinds of religious activities because of the joy they experience in them.

But there will come a time when God will bid them to go deeper. He will remove the previous consolation from the soul in order to teach it virtue and prevent it from developing vice .... Through the dark night, pride becomes humility, greed becomes simplicity, wrath becomes contentment, luxury becomes peace, gluttony becomes moderation, envy becomes joy, and sloth becomes strength. No soul will ever grow deep in the spiritual life unless God works passively in that soul by means of the dark night.

ST JOHN OF THE CROSS,
The Dark Night of the Soul

🦔 Have you ever experienced a 'dark night', when God's love and comfort seemed to have deserted you? Share your feelings with a Christian you sense is having a similar struggle.

Praise God for his help

IF God helps you in proportion to your problems, you should have no reason to complain, but rather, to bless his name.

ISAAC PENINGTON, *Letters on Spiritual Virtues*

❦ Have you noticed that God helps you in proportion to your problems? Praise him for it. Resolve to include similar praise in your daily prayers.

FATHER, once ... I had such big dreams, so much anticipation of the future. Now no shimmering horizon beckons me; my days are lacklustre. I see so little of lasting value in the daily round. Where is your plan for my life, Father?

You have told us that without vision we men perish. So Father in heaven, knowing that I can ask in confidence for what is your expressed will to give me, I can ask you to deposit in my mind and heart the particular dream, the special vision you have for my life.

And along with the dream, will you give me whatever graces, patience and stamina it takes to see the dream through to fruition? I sense that this may involve adventures I have not bargained for. But I want to trust you enough to follow even if you lead along new paths.

CATHERINE MARSHALL, *Adventures in Prayer*

&. Ask God to give you a dream, and the grace, patience and stamina to see it through to fruition.

Ask God to strengthen you

I am only a spark
Make me a fire.
I am only a string
Make me a lyre.
I am only a drop
Make me a fountain.
I am only an ant hill
Make me a mountain.
I am only a feather
Make me a wing.
I am only a rag
Make me a king!
MEXICAN PRAYER

🐾 Accept that without God you can do little. Ask him
to strengthen you, so that you can do more for him.

FOOTPRINTS on the sands of time are not made by sitting down.

ANONYMOUS

🐾 Think of something you could be doing for God today – and act upon it.

Believe in the impossible

FAITH consists in believing what is beyond the power of reason to believe. It is not enough that a thing be possible for it to be believed.

VOLTAIRE

❧ Does what you believe ever seem impossible to you? If so, remind yourself that to believe what seems unbelievable is true faith.

Don't blame others for difficulties

[DADDY] said: 'All children must look after their own upbringing.' Parents can only give good advice or put them on the right paths, but the final forming of a person's character lies in their own hands.

The Diary of Anne Frank

   Is there anyone you blame for your difficulties – physical, emotional or spiritual? Resolve to blame them no longer, and accept that your future attitude is up to you.

Believe the Bible is personal

WHEN you read God's word, you must constantly be saying to yourself, 'It is talking to me and about me.'
SØREN KIERKEGAARD

≥ Read a passage from the Bible, reminding yourself that it is talking to you and about you.

I think that when we are alone we sometimes see things a little bit more simply, more as they are. Sometimes when we are with others, especially when we are talking to others on religious subjects, we persuade ourselves that we believe more than we do.

FORBES ROBINSON, *Letters to His Friends*

🌿 How do your views about Christianity differ when you are alone to when you are talking to friends – both Christian and non-Christian? If there are differences, ask yourself why. Which views really represent what you think and feel?

Ponder on Christ's death

A ND can it be, that I should gain
An interest in the Saviour's blood?
Died he for me, who caused his pain –
For me, who him to death pursued?
Amazing love! How can it be
That thou, my God, shouldst die for me?
CHARLES WESLEY

❧ Read the crucifixion scenes in the gospels,
reminding yourself that Jesus went through
all that for you.

THERE is so much good in the worst of us,
And so much bad in the best of us,
That is hardly becomes any of us
To talk about the rest of us.

ANONYMOUS

🍂 Today, make a point of not saying a bad word
about anybody. Resolve to continue
throughout the week.

Be penitent

WHEN we want to make a gesture of our sorrow for what we have done or for the kind of people we are, we can do penance. Penance is one kind of gift that we can offer to God, and we choose to do it freely, because we want to make a gift. It is not a punishment that God inflicts on us.

MARGARET HEBBLETHWAITE,
Finding God in All Things

🍂 Make a self-sacrifice – e.g. abstain from watching TV, drinking alcohol or eating chocolate, visit a sick or elderly person – as a gesture of sorrow for something you have done or not done.

O H Lord my God! When I in awesome wonder
Consider all the works thy hand hath made
I see the stars, I hear the mighty thunder,
Thy power throughout the universe displayed.

Translated by STUART K. HINE

🍂 Look out at the morning or evening sky and
wonder at God's creative powers. Think of him
creating so much – and still caring, personally, for you.

Accept the road is hard — and easy

Yo u have noticed, I expect, that Christ himself sometimes describes the Christian way as very hard, sometimes as very easy. He says, 'Take up your cross' – in other words, it is like going to be beaten to death in a concentration camp. Next minute he says, 'My yoke is easy and my burden light.' He means both.

C. S. Lewis, *Mere Christianity*

In which ways have you found the Christian way easy to follow? In which ways have you found it to be very hard? Meditate on any lesson you can glean from this exercise.

See yourself as others see you

LORD, help me to face the truth about myself.
Help me to hear my words as others hear them, to see
  my face as others see me;
let me be honest enough to recognize my impatience
  and conceit;
let me recognize my anger and selfishness;
give me sufficient humility to accept my own
  weaknesses for what they are.
Give me the grace – at least in your presence – to say, 'I
  was wrong – forgive me.'

FRANK TOPPING

Take a look at yourself – your good qualities, your
bad qualities. What do the bad qualities say about you
to other people? What do they say about the extent of
your faith and Christian commitment?
Ask God for his forgiveness.

Be more like Jesus

FATHER, make us more like Jesus. Help us to bear difficulty, pain, disappointment and sorrow, knowing that in your perfect working and design you can use such bitter experiences to shape our characters and make us more like our Lord. We look with hope for that day when we shall be wholly like Christ, because we shall see him as he is. Amen.

MARY BATCHELOR

🙠 Read a passage about Jesus from the gospels. List his qualities. Pray that you will become more like him each day.

Celebrate variety

M Y faith was informed by a very simple observation: whenever I meditated on the work of God in creation I saw that God was about variety. It seemed that whenever God made something he did not make it in one or two but in hundreds and thousands of ways … different kinds of petals, schemes of thought, colours of skin, concepts of time, breeds of guinea pig, styles of music, senses of humour, types of planet; different cultures, different rain, different colours, different fabric, different alphabets, different light, different lettuce, different people. The world was bursting with God's abundance, from the solar systems outside our solar system to the atoms within matter; from the way in which people understood God to the spice they used in cooking.

JO IND, *Fat is a Spiritual Issue*

🐚 Look around you. What kinds of 'different' God-made things can you see? What does this tell you about God? Think about the different ways people interpret the Christian faith. Do you think God sees one interpretation as superior to another, or could Christians enjoy and learn from all of them?

Be alert

I saw a stranger today.
I put food for him in the eating-place
And drink in the drinking-place
And music in the listening-place.
In the Holy Name of the Trinity
He blessed myself and my house
My goods and family.
And the lark said in her warble
Often, often, often
Goes Christ in the stranger's guise
O, oft and oft and oft
Goes Christ in the stranger's guise.

ANONYMOUS

🍂 Be alert as you come into contact with strangers
today. By shunning them, are you shunning Christ?
By showing hospitality to them, are you showing
hospitality to Christ?

LOVING means to love the unlovable, or it is no virtue at all; forgiving means to pardon the unpardonable, or it is no virtue at all; faith means believing the unbelievable, or it is no virtue at all; and to hope means hoping when things are hopeless, or it is no virtue at all.

G. K. CHESTERTON

🔔 Try to get to know a person you find difficult to like or relate to. Work at loving them. Tell someone who wronged you that you forgive them.

See God as a loving parent

CAN it be possible that God loves human souls as much as I love my child – with this unutterable tenderness; with this longing pity, sympathy, comprehension; with this passion of desire to protect, supply, sustain? What would I not give my baby? Life's all, unhesitatingly! What would I not do if I but could? And he can.

And he says: 'Yes, they may forget,' even mothers, 'yet will I not forget thee.'

LUCY GUINNESS KUMM, *The Heart of Motherhood*

❧ Think of all the qualities of loving parenthood, of the things a mother and father would do for their child given the opportunity. Thank God for loving you in this way.

MAN cannot discover new oceans until he has courage to lose sight of the shore.

ANONYMOUS

🌢 What is preventing you from moving on to 'new oceans' – whether literally, spiritually or emotionally? Ask God to give you confidence to lose sight of your current, comfortable 'shore'.

'Feed' on God's word

MY spirit has become dry because it forgets to feed on you.

ST JOHN OF THE CROSS

🐾 When did you last 'feed' on God's word? Set aside some time today to read a passage from the Bible.

DEVOTION must be exercised in different ways by
the gentleman, the worker, the servant, the prince, the
widow, the young girl, and the married woman. Not
only is this true, but the practice of devotion must also
be adapted to the strength, activities, and duties of each
particular person .... True devotion ... not only does
no injury to one's vocation or occupation, but on the
contrary adorns and beautifies it. All kinds of precious
stones take on greater lustre when dipped into honey,
each according to its colour. So also every vocation
becomes more agreeable when united with devotion.
Care of one's family is rendered more peaceable, love
of husband and wife more sincere, service of one's
prince more faithful, and every type of employment
more pleasant and agreeable.

ST FRANCIS DE SALES,
Introduction to the Devout Life

❧ Which forms of devotion are best suited to your
character and work? Practise one of them today.
Praise God for your individuality.

Learn from Mary and Martha

To give our Lord a perfect hospitality, Mary and Martha must combine.

St Teresa of Avila

🐝 Read the story of Mary and Martha. Do you think you share mainly Mary's qualities, or Martha's? Start to work on acquiring the other's qualities as well.

A spiritual retreat is medicine for soul starvation. Through silence, solitary practice and simple living, we begin to fill the empty reservoir. This lifts the veils, dissolves the masks, and creates space within for the feelings of forgiveness, compassion and loving kindness that are often so blocked.

DAVID A. COOPER, *Silence, Simplicity and Solitude*

🍃 Think about going away for a retreat – perhaps even a short, one-day one. Look at your church notice-board or in your local library for information on retreat houses.

Accept yourself

In addition to trust in God, there will also emerge a trust in ourselves, a genuine belief in our own worth based not on endeavours but on the gift of being cherished …. We are acceptable to God because he is loving and merciful and not because we have done good things.

MYRA CHAVE-JONES, *Listening to Your Feelings*

🐚 Start to love and care about yourself, knowing that you are acceptable to God through grace rather than for being beautiful, wealthy, intelligent or talented.

Good can come from troubles

TROUBLES are often the tools by which God fashions us for better things.

HENRY WARD BEECHER

❧ What 'better things' have come out of your past troubles? Thank God for them – and remember them the next time troubles come your way.

Look for the improbable

I have seen flowers come in stony places
And kind things done by men with ugly faces
And the Gold Cup won by the worst horse at the races,
So I trust, too.

JOHN MASEFIELD

🍂 Think of something improbable that has happened in the world recently. Remind yourself of it when you are at a low ebb spiritually.

LORD, help me to remember that nothing is going to happen today that you and I together can't handle!

ANONYMOUS

🖋 Go confidently into a difficult situation knowing that you are not in it alone, but that you and God are in it together.

Wonder at God's love

AND I saw for certain, both here and elsewhere, that before ever he made us, God loved us; and that his love has never slackened, nor ever shall. In this love all his works have been done, and in this love he has made everything serve us; and in this love our life is everlasting. Our beginning was when we were made, but the love in which he made us never had beginning. In it we shall have our beginning.

ST JULIAN OF NORWICH,
Revelations of Divine Love

🦶 Thank God for loving you so much – even before you were born.

WE too often flog the Church when the whip should be laid on our own shoulders. We should always remember that we are a part of the Church, and that our own lack of revival is in some measure the cause of the lack of revival in the Church at large.

CHARLES SPURGEON, *Sermons*

Stop talking about revival in the Church, and pray earnestly for revival in your own life.

Accept you can't understand everything

CHRISTIAN revelation is clear, God is holy. God's ways are not our ways; God is wholly other and, thus, inaccessible to human understanding; the infinite cannot and may not be understood within finite categories. To live in a proper fear of God demands acknowledging and living in the face of this.

RONALD ROLHEISER, *The Shattered Lantern*

🙞 Accept that with our finite minds, nobody can really fully understand God and his ways. Praise him for this, accepting that if he could be fully understood, he would not be worth worshipping.

CHRIST alone is the leader of worship, and it is he who decides what is needed and when it is needed. We should recognize and welcome the free exercise of all the spiritual gifts, as they are used and directed by the Spirit.

RICHARD FOSTER, *A Celebration of Discipline*

🔔 Does Christ lead worship at your church, or is everything determined by the church's worship leader? Pray that everyone in your church will be open to the guidance of the Spirit – in worship, and in their own lives.

Be obedient

RETURNING to Holland after my release from the German concentration camp at Ravensbrück, I said, 'One thing I hope is that I'll never have to go to Germany again. I am willing to go wherever God may want me to go; but I hope he'll never send me to Germany.'

On my trips to the United States, I often spoke on the conditions in Europe during the post-war years, and when I talked of the chaos in Germany, people sometimes asked me, 'Why don't you go to Germany, since you know the language?' But I didn't want to go.

Then darkness came into my fellowship with God; when I asked for his guidance, there was no answer. Now God does not want us ever to be in doubt as to what his guidance is, and I knew that something had come between God and me, and I prayed, 'Lord, is there some disobedience in my life?' The answer was very distinct: 'Germany.'

'Yes, Lord, I'll go to Germany, too. I'll follow wherever you lead.'

CORRIE TEN BOOM, *Amazing Love*

❧ Ask God to show you if there is any disobedience in your life, which is coming between you and him. If there is, submit to his will for you.

BUT in coming to the Lord by means of 'praying the scripture', you do not read quickly; you read very slowly. You do not move from one passage to another, not until you have *sensed* the very heart of what you have read. You may then want to take that portion of scripture that has touched you and turn it into prayer.

After you have sensed something of the passage, and after you know that the essence of that portion has been extracted, and all the deeper sense of it is gone, then, very slowly, gently, and in a calm manner begin to read the next portion of that passage. You will be surprised to find that when your time with the Lord has ended, you will have read very little, probably no more than half a page.

MADAME GUYON,
Experiencing the Depths of Jesus Christ

🍂 Read a passage from the Bible *very slowly*. Don't move on until you have sensed every meaning from what it says.

Do all the good you can

Sins of omission are avoiding to do good of any kind when we have the opportunity. We must beware of these sins and, instead, be zealous of good works. Do all the good you possibly can to the bodies and souls of your neighbours. Be active. Give no place to laziness. Be always busy, losing no shred of time. Whatever your hand finds to do, do it with all your might.

John Wesley, *Christian Perfection*

🐾 Think of a good turn you can do for a neighbour today – e.g. mow their lawn, go to the shops, walk their dog. Act upon it.

IF every year we uprooted a single fault, we should soon become perfect.

THOMAS À KEMPIS, *The Imitation of Christ*

🐝 If you were to uproot one fault every year, which ones would you start with? Choose one of them and ask God to help you to be rid of it.

Be God's friend

THIS is true perfection: not to avoid a wicked life because like slaves we servilely fear punishment, nor to do good because we hope for rewards, as if cashing in on the virtuous life by some business-like arrangement. On the contrary, disregarding all those things for which we hope and which have been reserved by promise, we regard falling from God's friendship as the only thing dreadful and we consider becoming God's friend the only thing worthy of honour and desire. This, as I have said, is the perfection of life.

GREGORY OF NYSSA, *The Life of Moses*

  🍂 If Jesus walked through your door this minute, would he be proud to claim you as his friend? What can you do in your life to make such an outcome real?

Don't follow rules

ACCUSTOM yourself then, by degrees, thus to worship him, to beg his grace, to offer him your heart from time to time in the midst of your business, even every moment if you can. Do not always scrupulously confine yourself to certain rules, or particular forms of devotion, but act with a general confidence in God, in love and humility.

BROTHER LAWRENCE

Today, don't follow any rigid devotional 'rules' – e.g. having a Quiet Time at a certain time of day – but worship him whenever and wherever you can.

Follow God's desire

WHETHER contemplation, meditation, prayer, inward silence, intuition, quietude, or activity are what we wish for ourselves, the best is God's purpose for us at the present moment.

JEAN-PIERRE DE CAUSSADE,
The Sacrament of the Present Moment

❧ The next time you settle down for a habitual spiritual exercise (e.g. prayer, Bible study, silence), first ask God what *he* would like you to do at that moment.

WHOEVER truly loves you, good Lord,
walks in safety down a royal road, far from the
  dangerous abyss;
and if he so much as stumbles, you, O Lord, stretch
  out your hand.
Not one fall, or many, will cause you to abandon him if
  he loves you
  and does not love the things of this world
because he walks in the vale of humility.

ST TERESA OF AVILA

❧ Praise God that, however many times you may
'fall' from his ways, he will never abandon you. Try to
  imitate such loyalty in your own relationships.

See good in people

IN spite of everything, I feel that people are really good at heart.

The Diary of Anne Frank

❧ Today, look for good in everybody you meet.

THE teacher had advised them not to read Tolstoy novels because they were very long and would easily confuse the clear ideas which they had learned from reading critical studies of them.

ALEXANDER SOLZHENITSYN, *The First Circle*

For one week, close your ears to other people's theories about the Bible. Don't read any books about it, just read the Bible itself.

Change

GOD, help us to change. To change ourselves and to change our world. To know the need for it. To deal with the pain of it. To feel the joy of it. To undertake the journey without understanding the destination. The art of gentle revolution. Amen.

MICHAEL LEUNIG, *Common Prayer Collection*

🐚 Think of two things in your life you feel you should change. Ask God for the strength to change them.

PROGRESS is impossible without change; and those who cannot change their minds cannot change anything.

GEORGE BERNARD SHAW

෨ What attitude or issue is holding you back in your relationship with God or with other Christians? Ask God to help you let go of it.

Practise discipleship

ATTITUDES that define the disciple cannot be realized today by leaving family and business to accompany Jesus on his travels about the countryside. But discipleship can be made concrete by loving our enemies, blessing those who curse us, walking the second mile with an oppressor – in general, living out the gracious inward transformations of faith, hope and love. Such acts – carried out by the disciplined person with manifest grace, peace and joy – make discipleship no less tangible and shocking today than were those desertions of long ago.

DALLAS WILLARD, *The Spirit of the Disciplines*

🍃 Today, shock somebody by walking the second mile with someone you dislike.

BUT one thing that matters is that we always say 'yes' to God whenever we experience him, and really do will to be with him, with all our heart and soul and strength.

ST JULIAN OF NORWICH,
Revelations of Divine Love

🐝 Today, if God talks to you, agree to do his will, even if it is something you do not want to do.

Believe in the face of no evidence

I believe in the sun, even when it isn't shining;
I believe in love, even when I feel it not;
I believe in God, even when he is silent.
WORLD WAR TWO CONCENTRATION CAMP PRISONER
AWAITING EXECUTION

ॐ Think of something that you believe in – other
than God – which is intangible or apparently absent.
Remind yourself of this whenever you feel
God is no longer there.

WE nurse within our hearts the hope that we are different, that we are special, that we are extraordinary. We long for the assurance that our birth was no accident, that a god had a hand in our coming to be, that we exist by divine fiat. We ache for a cure for the ultimate disease of mortality. Our madness comes when the pressure is too great and we fabricate a vital lie to cover up the fact that we are mediocre, accidental, normal. We fail to see the glory of the Good News. The vital lie is unnecessary because all the things we long for have been given us freely.

ALAN JONES

🌢 Buy yourself and a friend a bunch of flowers or a box of chocolates to celebrate the fact that you are both special to God.

Think of the Church

NOTHING could more surely convince me of God's unending mercy than the continued existence on earth of the Church.

ANNE DILLARD, *Holy the Firm*

❧ Think of the turbulent times the Church as a whole has been through throughout history – even in recent years. Alongside that, ideologies and political ideas have come and gone. What does this say about what the Church believes?

Don't run away

HEAVENLY Father,
we are afraid of your light.
It is too searching, too bright, and we do not want its
beam upon our private life and secret thought.
We confess that we look for hiding places, and run even
into the night.
Nonetheless, search us out.
Shine your light upon us.
Expose our guilt and make us face it.
Bring us to the beckoning of your love.
Forgive us, and help us to bear your light.

More Contemporary Prayers, edited by Caryl Micklem

🐾 The next time you feel afraid to face God, ignore
the urge to flee and talk to him about why you want to
run away. Listen to his loving voice and experience
his forgiveness and grace.

Give up your life

HOW strange and unacceptable, the idea of giving up
   one's life in order to live.
And yet it is a fact borne out by experience.
The more inward looking I am, the more I hug my life
   to myself, the narrower my life becomes.
And the opposite is equally true.
I can see it in other people who give up their lives
   unreservedly to others, to a group, to a cause.
Their lives seem to open up and become filled with
   adventure and experience.
The secret is so simple, I am inclined to overlook it.
We are meant to live not merely with others, but for
   others.

FRANK TOPPING, *Wings of the Morning*

🐾 Is this true in your experience? Are you inward-
looking with a limited lifestyle, or outward-looking
with a varied lifestyle? If the former, ask God to show
you how you can give up your life and thus be
enriched by the experience.

Use your imagination

I imagine myself as the most wretched of all, full of sores and sins, and one who has committed all kinds of crimes against his king. Feeling a deep sorrow, I confess to him all of my sins, I ask forgiveness, and I abandon myself into his hands that he may do with me what he pleases.

The king, full of mercy and goodness, very far from chastening me, embraces me with love, invites me to feast at his table, serves me with his own hands, and gives me the key to his treasures. He converses with me, and takes delight in me, and treats me as if I were his favourite. That is how I imagine myself from time to time in his holy presence.

BROTHER LAWRENCE,
The Practice of the Presence of God

❧ Imagine a scene between yourself and God. What are you like? What is God like? How does such 'role play' help your faith?

Seek solitude

WITHOUT solitude, it is virtually impossible to lead a spiritual life. Solitude begins with a time and a place for God, and him alone. If we really believe not only that God exists but also that he is actively present in our lives – healing, teaching and guiding – we need to set aside a time and a space to give him our undivided attention. Jesus says, 'Go to your private room and, when you have shut the door, pray to the Father who is in that secret place.'

HENRI J. M. NOUWEN, *Making All Things New*

  Set aside a quiet, private place where you can retreat to pray when necessary. Make a habit of solitary prayer.

FASTING can bring breakthroughs in the spiritual realm that will never happen in any other way.

RICHARD FOSTER, *A Celebration of Discipline*

🐾 Try going without food for a few hours or a day and spend your meal-times in prayer.

Forgive the unforgivable

AT the close of a meeting in Berlin … a man came into the enquiry room. He appeared depressed and down-hearted and had great difficulty in saying what it was that troubled him so deeply. I became impatient with him, asking rather abruptly: 'Come along, what's your problem? I don't have much time. Let's talk together; perhaps I can help you?' His answer made me tremble.

'I was one of the guards at Ravensbrück,' he replied, 'during the time you were a prisoner there. A few months ago I was saved and brought all my sins to Jesus. He has forgiven me and I have prayed that I might be allowed to ask forgiveness from one of my victims …. Can you forgive me for my cruelties?'

At that moment it was as though a wave of God's love streamed through my heart, and I said to him, 'Brother, I forgive you with my whole heart!'

CORRIE TEN BOOM, *A Prisoner and Yet*

🐾 Has someone ever done something to you for which you find it impossible to forgive? Ask God to help you forgive them, recognizing that forgiveness releases the forgiver as well as the forgiven.

Learn from creation

E V E R Y flower of the field, every fibre of a plant, every particle of an insect, comes with the impress of its maker, and can – if duly considered – read us lectures of ethics or divinity.

SIR THOMAS POPE BLOUNT, *A Natural History*

🐚 Look closely at a plant or animal today. What does it teach you about its creator?

Thank God for his care

'LORD, you told me when I decided to follow you you would walk and talk with me all the way. But I'm aware that during the most troublesome times of my life there is only one set of footprints. I just don't understand why, when I needed you most, you leave me.'

He whispered, 'My precious child, I love you and will never leave you never, ever, during your trials and testings. When you saw only one set of footprints it was then that I carried you.'

MARGARET FISHBACK POWERS

❧ Recall the last time God carried you –
and thank him.

L ORD , give us weak eyes for things which are of no account and clear eyes for all your truth.

SØREN KIERKEGAARD

🔔 Today, focus on God's truth. Try to dismiss from your mind anything irrelevant to your walk with him.

Acknowledge 'burn-out'

ONE dear Christian expressed it to me this way: 'When I was first converted,' she said, 'I was so full of joy and love that I was only too glad and thankful to be allowed to do anything for my Lord, and I eagerly entered every open door. But after a while, as my early joy faded away, and my love burned less fervently, I began to wish I had not been quite so eager; for I found myself involved in lines of service that were gradually becoming very distasteful and burdensome to me.

'Since I had begun them, I could not very well give them up without exciting great remark, and yet I longed to do so increasingly. I was expected to visit the sick, pray beside their beds. I was expected to attend prayer meetings and speak at them. I was expected, in short, to be ready for every effort in Christian work, and the sense of these expectations bowed me down continually.'

HANNAH WHITALL SMITH,
The Christian's Secret of a Happy Life

🐾 Have you ever experienced similar Christian 'burn-out'? How did you come through it? Do you know anyone in this position you can pray for?

To quench thirst it is necessary to drink. Reading books about it only makes it worse.

JEAN-PIERRE DE CAUSSADE,
The Sacrament of the Present Moment

🐚 The next time you want to know more about God, don't pick up a book about it – approach God directly.

Put some work in

ONE general inlet to enthusiasm is expecting the end without the means: expecting knowledge, for instance, without searching the scriptures and consulting with the people of God, or expecting spiritual strength without constant prayer and steady watchfulness, or expecting God to bless you without hearing the word of God at every opportunity.

JOHN WESLEY, *Christian Perfection*

🐾 If you want God's blessing, think of ways you can work towards it – read the Bible more, pray more, act out your Christian values.

WHEN we live our lives correctly, we will see that all is gift. If we appropriate this, then our eyes will be opened and we will recognize that God has been walking on the road with us all along and we will say to each other, 'Were not our hearts burning within us as he spoke to us through all those experiences that we felt were only secular?'

RONALD ROLHEISER, *The Shattered Lantern*

🌢 As you go about your normal, secular activities today, look for evidence of God being with you in the middle of them.

Thank God for Jesus!

ETERNAL Father, we thank you for the life and teaching of Jesus. We thank you especially for the way he brought things to a head in people's lives, enabling them to discover that they could put their whole trust in you alone. Two thousand years later, the possibility of believing still comes as a crisis to us. Help us to face it, knowing that the decision whether or not to put faith in Jesus, and through him in you, is the greatest one of our lives.

More Contemporary Prayers, edited by Caryl Micklem

Praise God for Jesus' earthly ministry. Thank him for the way Jesus brought things to a head in your life. Ask him to help those who are currently putting their faith in Jesus. Ask him to help them to understand it is a major decision, the greatest of their life.

THE more I win thee, Lord,
The more for thee I pine;
Ah, such a heart of mine!

My eyes behold thee, and
Are filled and straight away then
Their hunger wakes again!

My arms have clasped thee and
Should set thee free, but no,
I cannot let thee go!

Lord Jesus Christ, beloved
Tell, O tell me true,
What shall thy servant do?

NARYAN VAMON TILCK

❧ Recognize when you're bored spiritually.
You should always be ready and willing to move on
in your Christian life. Look for ways that will
move you forward spiritually.

Pray every hour

I need thy presence, every passing hour;
What but thy grace can fill the tempter's power?
Who like thyself thy guide and staff can be?
Through cloud and sunshine, O, abide with me.
<small>HENRY FRANCIS LYTE</small>

❧ Today, remind yourself how much you need God's presence by praying, however briefly, at least once every waking hour.

Lo, Jesus meets us, risen from the tomb;
Lovingly, he greets us, scatters fear and gloom;
Let the church with gladness, hymns of triumph sing,
For her Lord now liveth, death has lost its sting.
Thine be the glory, risen conquering Son
Endless is the victory thou o'er death hast won.

EDMUND L. BUDRY

How would you feel if Jesus walked physically into your home today? How do you think your neighbours would feel if he walked down your street? How might you prepare yourself and your neighbours for such a meeting?

Be encouraged — and encourage

A<small>T</small> horse races the spectators intent on victory shout to their favourites in the contest, even though the horses are eager to run. From the stands they participate in the race with their eyes, thinking to incite the charioteer to keener effort, at the same time urging the horses on while leaning forward and flailing the air with their outstretched hands instead of a whip.

They do not do this because their actions themselves contribute anything to the victory; but in this way, by their goodwill, they eagerly show in voice and deed their concern for the contestants. I seem to be doing the same thing myself, most valued friend and brother. While you are competing in the divine race along the course of virtue, lightfootedly leaping and straining constantly for the prize of the heavenly calling, I exhort, urge and encourage you vigorously to increase your speed.

G<small>REGORY OF</small> N<small>YSSA</small>, *The Life of Moses*

🏵 Think of a person who has urged you on in your 'divine race'. Thank God for their encouragement. Now look around your fellowship for a young Christian whom you can encourage from the 'sidelines'.

Use your gifts

I began to see that the Holy Spirit never intended that people who had gifts and abilities should bury them in the earth, but rather, he commanded and stirred up such people to the exercise of their gift and sent out to work those who were able and ready.

JOHN BUNYAN,
Grace Abounding to the Chief of Sinners

🍂 Do you have a gift which you are hiding rather than using? Look for ways in which you can start to use it.

Play the game

FOR when the One Great Scorer comes
To write against your name,
He marks – not that you won or lost –
But how you played the game.
GRANTLAND RICE, *Alumnis Football*

🦶 Forget winning and losing in all aspects of your
faith – e.g. prayer life, evangelism, social outreach –
and remember that it's your motivation which is
important to God.

GOD is no more present in a church than in a drinking bar, but, generally, we are more present to God in a church than in a bar.

SHEILA CASSIDY, *Prayer for Pilgrims*

🕭 Drop into a church at some point today – focus your mind on God and pray.

Set your heart on the kingdom

THE spiritual life is a gift. It is the gift of the Holy Spirit, who lifts us up into the kingdom of God's love. But to say that being lifted up into the kingdom of love is a divine gift does not mean that we wait passively until the gift is offered.

Jesus tells us to set our hearts on the kingdom. Setting our hearts on something involves not only serious aspiration but also strong determination. A spiritual life requires human effort.

HENRI J. M. NOUWEN, *Making All Things New*

🐾 Think about the last time you really set your heart on something – a job, a college place, a romance. Remember how it occupied your thoughts and motivated your actions. Are you as zealous in pursuing your Christian faith?

I have found in many books many different ways of going to God and many different practices in living the spiritual life. I began to see that this was only confusing me, as the only thing I was seeking was to become wholly God's.

BROTHER LAWRENCE,
The Practice of the Presence of God

🐾 Have you ever felt confused by the – often conflicting – variety of advice in spiritual books? Decide not to read any more for a little while, and concentrate on finding your own, unique way to God.

Check your motivation

I F I go on a visit to the widows and fatherless, do I go purely on a principle of charity, free from any selfish views? If I go to a religious meeting, it puts me on thinking whether I go in sincerity and in a clear sense of duty, or whether it is not partly in conformity to custom, or partly from a sensible delight which my animal spirits feel in the company of other people, and whether to support my reputation as a religious man has no share in it.

JOHN WOOLMAN, *Journal*

❧ Ask yourself about your real motivation for attending church or carrying out Christian tasks. Is it because you love God, or is there another reason?

CONVERSION is a gift and an achievement. It is the act of a moment and the work of a lifetime.

E. STANLEY JONES, *Conversion*

🐚 How has your spiritual life progressed since you were converted? In which ways do you feel you haven't moved on? Why do you suppose this is? Ask God to strengthen you for future progression.

Be content

THE true Christian, whatever the misfortunes which providence heaps upon him, wants whatever comes and does not wish for anything which he or she does not have. The more one loves God, the more one is content.

FRANÇOIS FÉNELON, *Christian Perfection*

🐚 Make an inventory of the good things in your life and thank God for them. Then set aside any longings and ambitions and simply revel in where you are now or what you already have.

Clear away the rubbish

O thou great Chief, light a candle in my heart, that I may see what is therein, and sweep the rubbish from thy dwelling place.

AFRICAN SCHOOLGIRL'S PRAYER

🐾 What 'rubbish' could you do with throwing out of your life? Make a list and then, one by one, start throwing out the pieces, beginning today.

Find the best way

MY Father, teach us not only thy will, but how to do it. Teach us the best way of doing the best thing, lest we spoil the end by unworthy means.

REVD J. H. JOWETT

❧ If there is something you know God wants you to do for him, ask him to show you the best way of doing it. And be prepared to wait patiently for his answer.

IN order to be truthful we must do more than speak
   the truth.
We must also hear truth.
We must also receive truth.
We must also act upon truth.
We must also search for truth.
The difficult truth.
Within us and around us.
We must devote ourselves to truth.
Otherwise we are dishonest and our lives are mistaken.
God grant us the strength and the courage to be
   truthful.
Amen.

MICHAEL LEUNIG, *Common Prayer Collection*

🙠 Ask God to help you discern when people around
   you are telling the truth. Respond to it when you
            find it and help to proclaim it.

Everywhere is holy

JESUS, where'er thy people meet
Where they behold thy mercy seat
Where'er they seek thee thou art found
And every place is hallowed ground.

WILLIAM COWPER

❧ Remember that everywhere you meet with God
becomes holy ground. Jesus is not confined
to church buildings!

Acknowledgements

My thanks are due to the following people who either directly or indirectly helped me to compile this book: members of the Endowed Mission Hall in Rowley Regis who kindly lent me various spiritual classics; Bruce Clift and Jane Foulkes for introducing me to other useful books; my parents Vera and Richard Round and then-fiancé (now my husband), Grant Filleul who gave me space in which to work; and Christine Smith, editorial director of Marshall Pickering, for her help and encouragement, and for commissioning me in the first place.

The acknowledgements pages constitute an extension of the copyright pages.

Abingdon Press, for excerpts from the following:
1. *Conversion* by E. Stanley Jones.
2. *Christian Perfection* by John Wesley.

Bantam Doubleday Dell Publishing Group, for excerpts from *Introduction to the Devout Life* by Francis de Sales.

Friends United Press, for excerpts from *Prayer and Worship*, by Douglas V. Steere.

HarperCollins, for excerpts from the following:
1. *The Sacrament of the Present Moment* by Jean-Pierre de Caussade.
2. *Reflections on the Christian Life* by François Fénelon.
3. *Footprints* by Margaret Fishback Powers.
4. *Finding God in All Things* by Margaret Hebblethwaite.
5. *Mere Christianity* by C. S. Lewis.
6. *Making All Things New* by Henri Nouwen.
7. *The Spirit of the Disciplines* by Dallas Willard.

HarperCollins *Religious*, Melbourne, Australia for excepts from *Common Prayer Collection* by Michael Leunig.

Hodder and Stoughton, for excerpts from the following:
1. *A Celebration of Discipline* by Richard Foster.
2. *The Shattered Lantern* by Ronald Rolheiser.
3. *A Journey into God* by Delia Smith.

Lion Publishing, for excerpts from the following:
1. 'Prayer' by Mary Batchelor, from *The Lion Prayer Collection*.
2. *Listening to Your Feelings* by Myra Chave-Jones.

Lutterworth Press, for excerpts from *Wings of the Morning* by Frank Topping.

Macmillan Publishing Company and Oxford University Press, for excerpts from *A Diary of Private Prayer* by John Baillie.

Mowbray, for excerpts from *Fat is a Spiritual Issue* by Jo Ind.

Thomas Nelson Inc., for excerpts from *The Imitation of Christ* by Thomas à Kempis, translated by E. M. Blaiklock.

New Reader's Press, for excerpts from *Letters by a Modern Mystic* by Frank Laubach.

Penguin Books, for excerpts from the following:
1. *The Fire of Love* by Richard Rolle.
2. *Revelations of Divine Love* by Julian of Norwich.

SCM Press, for excerpts from *More Contemporary Prayers* edited by Caryl Micklem.

All Bible quotations are taken from the NRSV.

Every effort has been made to trace copyright owners, and the author and publisher apologize to anyone whose rights have inadvertently not been acknowledged. This will be corrected in any reprint.